Songs For Meditation

Kenneth P. Langer

Brass Bell Books

BRASS BELL
BOOKS & GAMES

Published by Brass Bell Books and Games
www.brassbellbooks.com

Printed in the United States of America

Contents

Songs for Meditation

by

Kenneth P. Langer

Introduction

This book is a collection of fifty original songs that can be used for meditation and spiritual work. Each song contains at least a single line of music with words. All the songs can be done by one singer or by a lead singer with a group of others. Many of the songs can be done as a round and some use a technique known as call and response. All the songs are meant to have a melody that is easy to learn and remember. Though many of the songs are only a single line some have additional lines of easy music that can be done along with the main melody. These possibilities give song leaders a great deal of flexibility in using them with different groups of singers.

What Is Singing Meditation?

Singing meditation is a spiritual practice that can be done by one person or a group of people. The practice is to enter a state of meditation through the repetitive singing of a song. The repetition of the music allows the practitioner to memorize the music and continue to sing it until the vibrations of the sound and the repetition of the melody bring the mind to an altered state. It is similar to the practice of repeating a mantra or moving through a tai chi form.

These songs were composed because I have led singing meditation groups and have found it difficult to find appropriate songs to use. I needed simple songs that could be easily learned and that reflected different religious and spiritual principles. In singing meditation groups participants are encouraged not just to learn the song and sing along but can also add counterpoint (if it is a round) or to improvise. Participants are also welcome to just listen, move, hum, or participate however they wish.

My singing meditation groups sessions usually begin with an introduction to the practice then start off with the toning of a single note as a way to enter into the spirit of meditation and to warm up the voice. Next, an opening song is introduced and a candle is lit. Most all the songs are sung 7-10 times and are then followed by a moment of contemplative silence. After the opening chant about five more songs are done in the same manner until the closing chant is performed and the candle is extinguished. The opening and the closing chant are the same for each session while the middle songs change each time.

The Songs

1. Aham Prema

"Aah-ham-pree-mah"

I am divine love (Sanskrit)

Kenneth Langer

A - ham pre - ma. A - ham pre - ma.

A - ham pre - ma. A - ham Pre - ma. Om

2. All In One

adapted from a text by Seng Ts'an, Buddhist Monk

Kenneth Langer

3. All You Are

adapted from the Dhammapada

Kenneth Langer

All you are is what you think. What you think is what you say.

What you say is what you do. What you do is who you are. Oh,

4. Become Another

original text

Kenneth Langer

Be not a seek - er of things; Be -
come a seek - er of jus - tice. Be not a lo - ver of
ob - jects; Be - come an ob - ject of love. Be
not the one who needs; be not the one who
wants. Be - come the one who wants to help those in need.

5. Blessed Are They

adapted from the Gospel of Matthew "Sermon on the Mount"　　　　　　　Kenneth Langer

Bles - sed   are   those   who   mourn   for

Bles - sed   are   those   in   pain   for

Bles - sed   are   those   in   need   for

Bles - sed   are   those   of   peace   for

Bles - sed   are   those   of   truth   for

Bles - sed   are   those   who   seek   for

Blessed Are They - 2

they shall find com-fort.

they shall find strength.

they shall be filled.

they shall be sac-red.

they shall be hon-ored.

they shall find peace.

6. Breathing Meditation

original text

Ken Langer

Brea - thing in,   I'm filled with
Brea - thing in,   I'm filled with
Brea - thing in,   I'm filled with

Brea - thing in,
Brea - thing in,
Brea - thing in,

peace.   Brea-thing out,   I send out
love   Brea-thing out,   I send out
hope   Brea-thing out,   I send out

I'm filled with peace.   Brea-thing out,
I'm filled with love   Brea-thing out,
I'm filled with hope   Brea-thing out,

love.   Brea - thing
hope   Brea - thing
peace.   Brea - thing

I send out love.
I send out hope.
I send out peace.

7. Child Of Light

adapted from a text by Aberjhani

Kenneth Langer

You were born a child of light. Its sec-rets will shine in your life. Then you will re-turn to the beau-ty that was al-ways you.

(last time)

8. Cross The River

adapted from the Dhammapada

Kenneth Langer

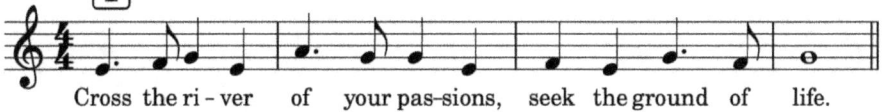

Cross the ri - ver of your pas-sions, seek the ground of life.

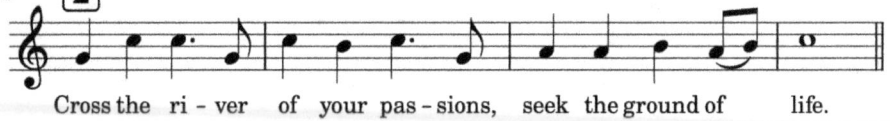

Cross the ri - ver of your pas - sions, seek the ground of life.

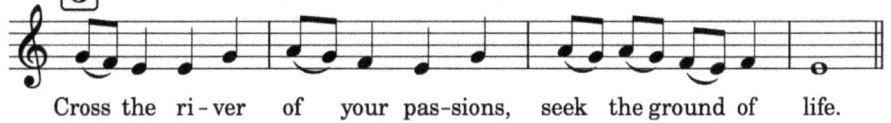

Cross the ri - ver of your pas-sions, seek the ground of life.

Cross the ri - ver, seek the ground of life.

9. Dawn Appears

adapted from a Hindu chant by Sri Chinmoy

Kenneth Langer

Gra-dual-ly, soft and slow (oh)

The vir-gin dawn ap - pears. with-in the ve - ry

depth of - my heart.

10. Empty Of Things

adapted from a text by Hadewijch

Kenneth Langer

If you emp-ty your mind of things it can be
filled with wis - dom. If you emp-ty your heart of
things it can be filled with beau - ty. If you
emp-ty your soul of things it can be filled with such
sa - cred - ness. If you emp-ty your soul of things it can be
filled with love. If you

11. Find The Peace

adapted from the Tao Te Ching

Kenneth Langer

1 Find the peace with - in.

2 Hold on to the still - ness.

3 And you shall mas - ter the

4 ten thou - sand things.

12. Follow The Sound

original text

Kenneth Langer

Fol - low the sound
Fol - low the pain,
Seek out the light,
Live in the heart,

Fol - low the sound oh, Fol - low the sound oh,
Fol - low the pain oh, Fol - low the pain oh,
Seek out the light oh, Seek out the light oh,
Live in the heart oh, Live in the heart oh,

fol - low the sound Hear it call you,
fol - low the pain. Go where it leads you,
seek out the light shin - ing with - in and
live in the heart. Find where it guides you,

Fol - low the sound oh, Fol - low the sound oh,
Fol - low the pain oh, Fol - low the pain oh,
Seek out the light oh, Seek out the light oh,
Live in the heart oh, Live in the heart oh,

from all a - round. Fol - low its trail to the
call out its name. Fol - low its trail to the
shin - ing out-right. Fol - low its beam to the
right from the start. Fol - low its warmth and you'll

Fol - low the sound oh, Fol - low the sound oh,
Fol - low the pain oh, Fol - low the pain oh,
Seek out the light oh, Seek out the light oh,
Live in the heart oh, Live in the heart oh,

Follow The Sound - 2

top of the hill and in its space let your
mouth of the cave and in its space let your
depths of the night and in its space let your
not be a-lone and in its space let your

Fol-low the sound oh, Fol-low the sound oh,
Fol-low the pain oh, Fol-low the pain oh,
Seek out the light oh, Seek out the light oh,
Live in the heart oh, Live in the heart oh,

soul be filled.
soul be saved.
soul be bright.
soul be known.

Fol - low the sound.
Fol - low the pain.
Seek out the light.
Live in the heart.

13. Forget

text adapted from Kamand Kojouri, Sufi Poet

Kenneth Langer

For - get your voice and sing. For - get your feet and

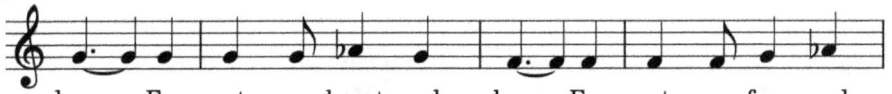

dance. For - get your heart and love. For - get your fear and

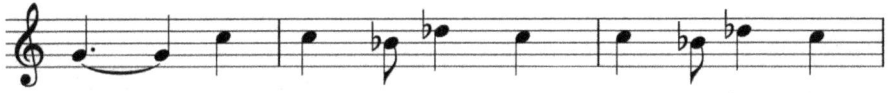

laugh. For - get your life, let go of life, for -

get your life and live. For - get your-self and be.

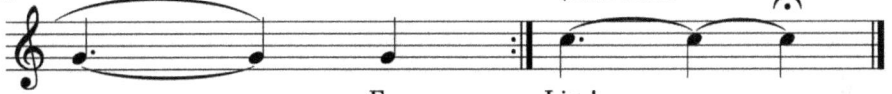

(Last Time

For Live!
(Just)

19

14. Gate To Freedom

adapted from a Zen text by Huang Po

Kenneth Langer

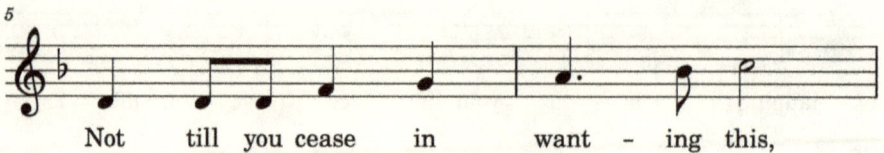

Not till your thoughts cease run - ning here, run - ning there, e - very-where. Not till you cease in want - ing this, want - ing that, e - very-thing will you find the gate to free - dom.

15. Go In Peace

Call and Response

Kenneth Langer

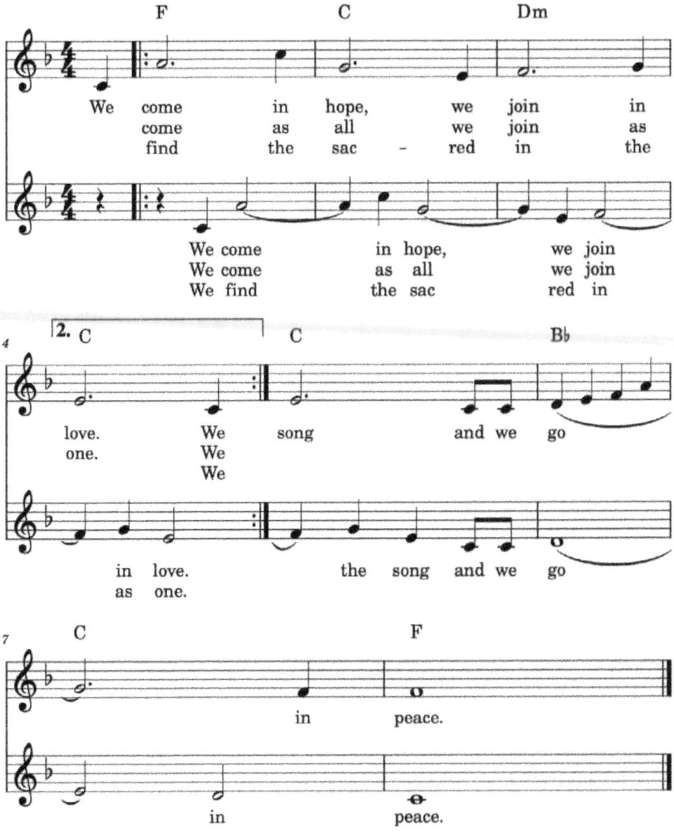

16. I Am Love

adapted from Hildegard of Bingen

Kenneth Langer

I am in your midst. who-e - ver

knows me can ne-ver fall. Not in the heights, not

in the depths, nor in the breadths for I am love.

17. I It Am

text by Julian of Norwich

Kenneth Langer

1 I it am the great-ness and good-ness of the fa-ther.

2 I it am the wis-dom and kind-ness of the mo-ther.

3 I it am, I it am.

18. In A Quiet Moment

In a qui - et mo - ment, ah

In a qui - et mo - ment, ah

In a qui - et mo - ment, ah

dee dee dee dee dee dee dee dee dee dee dee

la la la la la la la la la la

ah ah

soft - ness en - ters in. ah

soft - ness en - ters in - ah

soft - ness en - ters in.

dee dee dee dee dee dee dee dee dee dee dee

la la la la la la la la

ah ah

In A Quiet Moment - 2

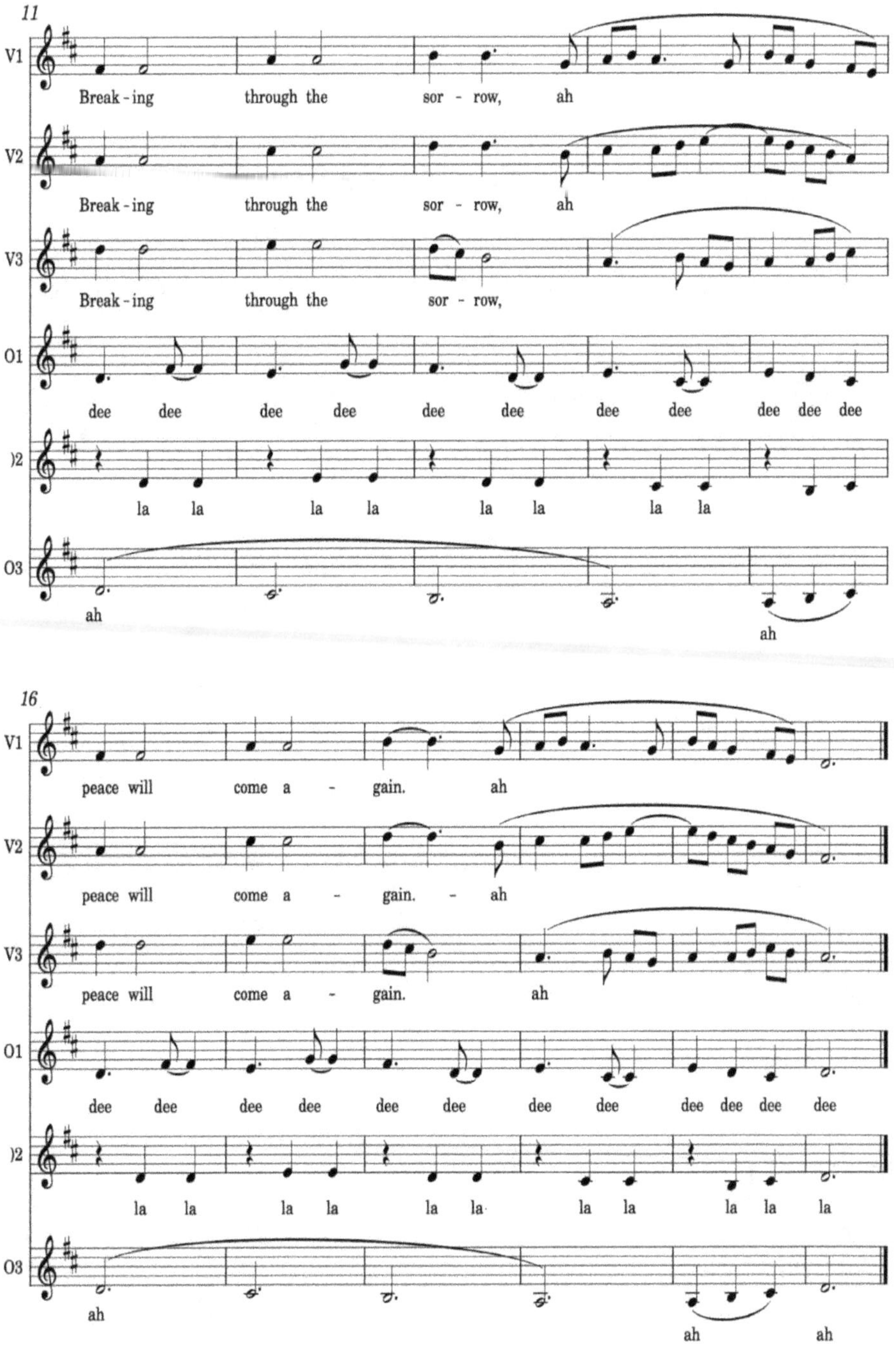

19. Increase My Light

adapted from Muhammed's Prayer of Light

Kenneth Langer

Grant me light in my heart, grant me light in my ears, grant me light in my eyes, grant me light in my soul. Grant me light in my words. Grant me light from a - bove, grant me light from be - low, grant me light from with - in. Grant me

Ostinato 1

In - crease my - light.

Ostinato 2

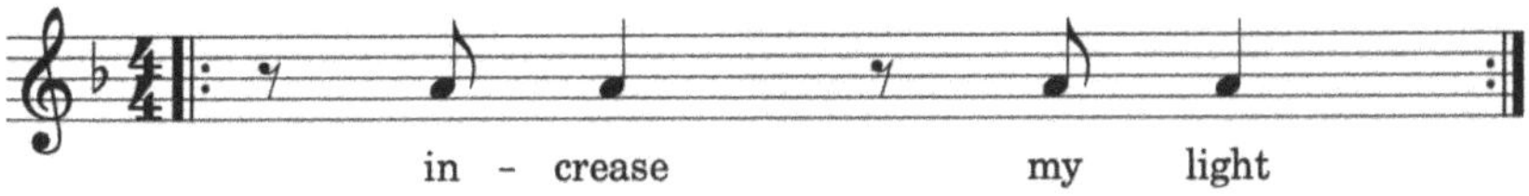
in - crease my light

20. Invisible One

adapted from the Kena Upanishad

Kenneth Langer

The self is the ear of the

The self

ear, the eye of the

is the ear of the ear,

eye, the mind of the mind. The

the eye of the eye, the mind of the mind.

self is the word of the words and the life of

The self is the word of the words

Invisible One - 2

life. Ri-sing a-bove the sen-ses,

and the life of life. Ri-sing a-bove the sen-ses,

reach-ing a-bove the mind and re - noun-cing se - parate ex - ist-ence we

reach-ing a-bove the mind and re - noun-cing se - parate ex - ist-ence

find the e - ter - nal self.

we find the e - ter - nal self.

21. Let Me Walk In Beauty

adapted from a text by Chief Yellow Lark

Kenneth Langer

Let me walk in beau-ty. Let my eyes be-hold the sun-set. Let my ears hear your voice, Oh Great Spi - rit. O, Great Spi - rit.

22. Let My Soul Be Free

inspired from an Iglulik Eskimo poem

Kenneth Langer

[1]

Take me to the ri - ver. Car-ry me to the sea.

Take me to the ri - ver. Oh,

Take me to the

Let me breathe the o - cean. Let my soul be free. Oh,

take me to the o - cean.

mount - - tain.

Let My Soul Be Free - 2

Take me to the mount-ain, Lift me up to the sky.

Take me to the moun - tain. Oh,

Fill my heart with

Fill my heart with love and hope. Let my soul fly high.

fill me with love and hope.

love and hope.

23. Let Your Heart Speak

original text

Kenneth Langer

Come in-to si - lence, come in-to peace. Come in-to

gra - ti - tude and let all ang - er cease. Claim sa - cred

ground, seek what you seek. O-pen your heart and let it speak.

24. Let There Be Room

adapted from a text by Pema Chodron

Kenneth Langer

Let there be room, for not know-ing. Let the path re-veal it-self. Let the path re-veal it-self. Let, Let there be room for not want-ing.

Let, let there be room to grow. Let the path re-veal it-self. Let, let there be room to grow.

34

Let There Be Room - 2

25. Litany To The Saints

original text

Kenneth Langer

(recite names) (leader) ,(group

Ah   We   praise those who   come be-fore. We

praise   thee, *(we   praise thee)*   we   praise   thee, *(we*

praise *thee)*   we   sing   our   praise   to   you.

Possible names to recite:

"Jesus, the Buddha, and Confucius are a few.

Mohammad, Lao Tzu, and Abraham are too."

"William Ellery Channing, Ralph Waldo Emerson, and Theodore Parker are a few.

Jane Addams, Susan B. Anthony, and Harriet Tubman are too."

"Thomas Jefferson, Thomas Paine, and Roger Williams are a few. Abraham Lincoln, Gandhi, and Martin Luther King Jr. are too."

26. Lord Make Me An Instrument

adapted from St. Francis of Assisi

Kenneth Langer

(all together)

Lord, make me an in-str-ment of thy peace.

(call and response)

Where there is hat - red, there is love.

Where there is in - ju - ry: there is par - don.

Where there is doubt: there is faith.

Where there is des - pair: there is hope.

Where there is sad - ness: there is joy.

27. Love As You Love

original text

Kenneth Langer

Love as you love. Live as you live.

Be as you are in love. If you move in

peace then you'll have no fear. With com - pas - sion

will your way be clear.

28. Lumen De Lumine

Latin chant

Kenneth Langer

Lu – men de   Lu – mi – ne.   Lu – min de   Lu – mi – ne.

Lu – min   de   Lu – mi – ne.

29. Many Stories

original text

Kenneth Langer

Let's build a world with words from ma - ny sto - ries, sung by ma-ny voi - ces, heard by ma - ny hearts and weave them in to the fab - ric of peace, the fab - ric of peace.

30. Mirror

adapted from a text by Mahmud Shabestari

Kenneth Langer

With - in each a-tom is a thou - sand suns. With -

in each rain-drop is a thou - sand streams. With -

in each peb-ble is a thou - sand seeds With -

in each seed is the u - ni - verse. With -

in each heart is the sa - cred.

31 Most Noble Greenness

(adapted from a text by Hildegard of Bingen)   Kenneth Langer

O most no - ble Green-ness, root-ed in the

sun, and who shines in bright se - re - ni - ty u-

pon the wheel, No-thing on the earth can

com - pre - hend you, you are en - cir - cled in the

arms of di - vine my - ster - y

32. O Let Us

original text   Kenneth Langer

Part 1

Oh,   let   us   have   po - wer   to
       let   us   have   cour - age   to
       let   us   have   strength   to

see   past   di - vi - sions and   let   us   have
with - stand   the   hat   tred   and   let   us   have
make   us   be   fear   less   and   let   us   have

po - wer   to   lift   up   the   peo - ple.   Oh,
cour - age   to   act   with - out   ang - er.   Oh,
strength   to   do   what   is   need - ed.   Oh,

Part 2

let   us   be u - ni - ted   and   seek the   truth in   just - ice.   Oh,

Part 3

Sing   in   hope   as   one   peo   ple,   one   peo - ple.

44

33. Om Mani Padme Hum

Buddhist chant

Kenneth Langer

Om ma-ni pad-me hum. Om ma-ni pad-me hum.

Om ma-ni pad - me hum. Om ma-ni pad-me hum.

34. On Love

adapted from "The Epistle of Love" by St. Paul

Kenneth Langer

If I claim the truth but have not love, I have no-thing.

If I claim true faith but have not love, I have no -

thing. If I give my - self but have not love I have

(last time)

no - thing. If I

35. One In Us

adapted from the Gospel of John 17:21

Kenneth Langer

That we may all be one. Just as

you are in me and I am in you. May

we be one in us.

36. Open The Window

(original text)

Kenneth Langer

Beau – ty sur – rounds you,
Lo – ving sur – rounds you,
Won – der sur – rounds you,

beau – ty a-bounds in you from up a – bove
lo – ving a-bounds in you from up a – bove
won-der a-bounds in you from up a – bove

to down be – low. When beau-ty seems lost
to down be – low. When all love seems lost
to down be – low. When won-der seems lost

it can be found a-gain, o-pen the win-dow and let it in.
it can be found a-gain, o-pen the win-dow and let it in.
it can be found a-gain, o-pen the win-dow and let it in.

Open The Window - 2

Beau - ty and peace are found e - very - where, so
Pure love and hope are found e - very - where, so
Pure Joy and awe are found e - very - where, so

o - pen the win - dow and let them in.
o - pen the win - dow and let them in.
o - pen the win - dow and let them in.

37. Peace Comes From Oneness

Adapted from a text by Black Elk

Kenneth Langer

1 Peace comes from one-ness. O, Great Spi - rit.

2 One-ness dwells at the cen-ter. Oh, Great Spi - rit. The

3 cen-ter is found e - very-where. O Great Spi - rit. The

4 cen - ter is in e - very heart.

5 Find the sac - red peace. (last time)

38. Sacred Garden

adapted from a poem by Kabir

Kenneth Langer

Though you seek the sac - red gar - den

on the path of where you've been, you shall find the

sac - red gar - den wait - ing there from deep with - in.

Take a seat a - mong the flow - There you will find your

sac - red place. Take a seat a - mong the flow-ers and

there be filled by their grace.

39. Salutations

adapted from Hindu chant "Devi Suktam"   Kenneth Langer

Sal - u - ta - tions to God dess who

lives with - in e-very one of us. Sal - u - ta - tions,

sal - u - ta - tions, sal - u - ta - tions to her a-gain.

and a - gain.

40. Satchitananda

adapted from a Hindu concept

Kenneth Langer

Sat, chit, a - nan - da.

Be - ing, con - scious - ness, and bliss.

Sat, chit, a - nan - da.

Be - ing, con - scious - ness, and bliss.

41. See The World

adapted from a poem by William Blake

Kenneth Langer

See the world in a grain of sand and hea-ven in a wild flo-wer. Hold for - ev - er in your hand and e ter - ni-ty in a mo - ment, a sing - gle mo - ment.

42. Shine On

adapted from the poetry of Aberjhani

Kenneth Langer

Shine On - 2

Shine On - 3

Shine On - 4

26
M
CM
R1
R2
R3
Be filled.
Shine on Shine on Shine on Be
Shine on and on. Shine on and on. Shine on and on. Be,
on. Shine on. Be filled with

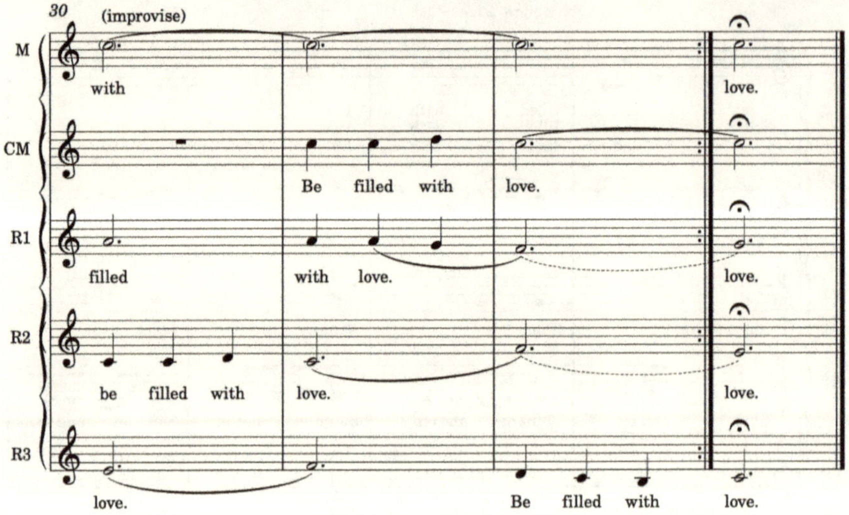
30
(improvise)
M
CM
R1
R2
R3
with love.
Be filled with love.
filled with love. love.
be filled with love. love.
love. Be filled with love.

43. Speak The Truth

(original text)

Kenneth Langer

Speak the truth! Speak it bold - ly, ne - ver fear.

Speak it out loud so that all may hear. Break - ing

through the hate and fear. Speak the truth.

44. Still World

adapted from the Tao Te Ching

Kenneth Langer

1 The Tao does no-thing, yet ev-ery-thing is done. If

2 we would grasp this, we would be trans-formed. Re

3 turn to sim - pli - ci - ty, no need for de-sire

4 Then there is peace and the world is still.

45. The Mirror

adapted from a text by Hadewijch II

Kenneth Langer

You who want know-ledge see the one-ness with - in.

There waits the re - flec-tion from where you be - gin. The

truth is with - in.

46. There Is You

adapted from words by Levi Yitzchak of Berditchov

Kenneth Langer

Where I wan - der there is you.

Where I pon - der there is you. Where I go there is

you. On - ly you e-very - where. All the sky is

you. All the earth is you. and with-in me you are

there. On - ly you e-very - where. where. On-ly

you, e - very where. On - ly you.

47. Weather The Storm

adapted from a text by Nayyirah Waheed

Kenneth Langer

If the o - cean wa - ters

If the o - cean can find

can find peace, so can you. Oh,

peace, so can you. Oh,

If the des - ert wind storms

If the wind storms can find

Weather The Storm - 2

can find peace, so can you. You are

peace, so can you. You are

salt wa - ter mixed with air. You are

wa - ter mixed with air. You are

moist breath warmed by the sun. Find your

moist breath warmed by the sun. Find your

true self and wea - ther the storm.

true self and wea - ther the storm.

48. What Lives Within

adapted from a text by Henry David Thoreau

Kenneth Langer

What lies be - hind us and what lies a - head are ti - ny mat - ters from what lives with - in.

49. Winter Solstice

(original text)

Kenneth Langer

1 In the midst of dark - ness we are still, we are still.
2 In the midst of fros - ty winds we are still, we are still.
3 As we wait for the re - birth of the sun's light. Oh come might - y sun -

Last Time

light. In the light. Oh come.

50. You Do For All

(adapted from the Gospel of Mathew)

Kenneth Langer

What you do for the least of them,

What you do for the least of them,

for your sis-ters, for your bro-thers.

for your sis-ters, for your bro-thers.

What you do for the least of us, you

What you do for the least of us,

do for me, you do for all.

you do for me, you do for all.

www.ingramcontent.com/pod-product-compliance
Lightning Source LLC
La Vergne TN
LVHW041207080426
835508LV00008B/843